Best Wishes

Always

All Houlan

2008

Reflections

Sharing Thoughts One-on-One

Alvin M. O'Hanlon

Phoenix Press
Fort Lauderdale, Florida

Library of Congress
Catalog Card Number : 86-061409

ISBN : 0-9616898-0-3

Dedication

This book is dedicated to every person who is hurting.

acknowledgements

Danny Atchley
Lehigh, Florida
cover design

Wendy Gould
Delray Beach, Florida
calligraphy

Betty Wright
Moore Haven, Florida
publishing consultant

During my 50 plus years of life, and especially the 20 that I have been running as a form of exercise, I have done a lot of thinking about many things. The thinking has let me extract from my observations and experiences brief philosophical "Reflections" which I have used to guide me as I encountered life's new situations. This has allowed me to have a more peaceful and happier life. During discussions with others, some of my "Reflections" worked their way into the conversation and I frequently have been asked if I ever intended to do any writing.

Thus, the following...

Above all else,
know
yourself,
for you are
the most important
person in your
life.

Most things
in life
are
relative
inasmuch as
there are
very few,
if any,
absolutes.

The wealth I
have acquired
in life is
the friends
I have made,
the love I
have shared,
and the
peace
within my
soul.

We should
never
set out
to destroy
anything
that is good
and
wholesome.

We tend
to interpret
others
in terms
of our
own
motivations
and
self
image.

Accept
yourself,
since
no one
is
flawless.

If you
    look at
life in the
light of
    yesterday,
do not get
    lost
    in the
shadows
it casts.

Material
things
tend to
control
you more
than
you
control
them.

When I am like
I am now,
I wonder how
I could have
ever been
different.
When I am
different than
I am now, I
wonder how
I could have ever
been like I am now.

Emotional,
as well as
physical,
injury
has a
period of
healing which
cannot be
significantly
altered.

We should
only
compare
ourself
to
ourself.

Sometimes,
freedom
creates
loneliness
as well as
aloneness.

Do not
  take away
anything
  you cannot
  give back.

The distances
do not get
any shorter, nor
do the
weights get
any lighter;
but they
seem to as
we gain
speed and
strength.

People,
situations,
and things
are to be
recognized by
their
substance and
form and
not by what
they are
claimed to be.

Have
no fear
of loving
or being
loved.

Our most
dangerous
enemy is our
own mouth.
We must
be very careful
what we
put in it,
and what
we let come out
of it.

Do not
confuse
disappointment
with
unhappiness.

Always
leave a
person
an excuse to
be used.

Being alone
is a
physical state
and loneliness
is a mental
state and
the two do
not always
coexist.

A drowning
person
doesn't care
who is
throwing
the
lifeline.

The problem
with
conventional
thinking
is that it
is limited
by convention
and will
only produce
conventional
results.

A relationship should
be self defining,
much as the course
of a stream
is defined by
the communion
of the water with
the terrain
over which it
flows.

The
first
commitment
one
should
make is
to
oneself.

Peace
within
your soul
is the
basis for
any real
wealth.

The cost
of freedom
can be the
foregoing
of
relationships,
both
personal
and
financial.

Curiosity
produces
more
questions
than
answers.

Happiness
starts
with a
healthy
respect for
yourself.

Love is
the
unqualified,
unilateral
caring
of
one for
another.

World peace
will not
be achieved
until
greed is
eliminated
from the
human
race.

If you do
not want
to hear the
answer,
do not ask
the
question.

We must
periodically
reteach
ourselves
the
important
lessons
of life.

If you have
a problem,
look for
the simplest
solution
first.
Usually that
is where
the answer
is.

How can
any society
enter into
a thought
process for
the purpose
of deciding how
to humanely
kill a
human being.

Finding
fault with
others
neither justifies
your mistakes,
nor solves
your problems.

Because
I love you
does not mean
that I
must impale
myself
on the
emotion.

The path
to happiness
is obvious once
we have
developed the
perception
that enables us
to see it
and the will
that enables
us to
follow it.

Unless you are
able to accept the
consequence
of a discovery,
do not set
out to make it.

Inner peace
is the
bedrock
of
happiness.

If peace in
the world
is to be
achieved, it
must be
started on an
individual
basis, one
person to
another, and
grow from there.

The hallmark
of a secure
person is the
desire to
discover
the future
rather than
continually
visit the
past.

If a
relationship
demands
possession,
it is
greed, not
love.

Those who
have
mastered
life will
use the
force of
anything set
against
them to their
own advantage.

To not allow
one to seek
their own way
in life is to
cut the
stem of a
beautiful white
flower when
the bud
first appears.

I am the
most
significant
person in
my life.
I hope you are
the most
significant
person in
your life.

It does not matter
who gets credit;
what does matter is
that the job gets
done.

Knowledge is
ethereal rather
than physical
but is there
for us to
find, just
like an
undiscovered
physical object.

It is usually
a long road to
any worthwhile
achievement.

Reality is
both fact
and perception;
but when
fact and
perception
are the

same,
you then
have truth.

Do not let
anxiety about
the future destroy
the sweetness of
the present.

Enter a
person's life
as gently as
a feather
floats to
the ground.

Being an
anchor is
not easy.

Understanding
why you
hurt
doesn't in
and of
itself
make the
pain
go away.

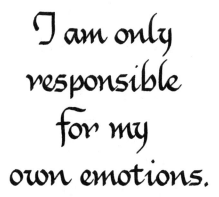

I am only
responsible
for my
own emotions.

Hurting you
is no
solution to
the
perception
that you
have hurt
me.
The solution
is understanding
each other's
fears and needs.

The best
investment
you can
make is
in
yourself.

It seems
like
everyone
is a
slave to
something.

A champion
is a person
who does
what has to
be done when
it has to be
done.

Love
is not
mutually
exclusive.

I almost always
never understand you,
but I always
love you.

Abuse is
the precursor
of laws and
revolutions.

Normally,
    when one jumps
to a conclusion it
    is usually wrong,
    as well as
    the worst
possible appraisal
of the situation
    or person.

Never be
afraid to
express a
thought or
feeling if it
springs forth
from your
soul.

Life exists
as we
choose to
perceive it.

However
difficult,
there may be
a time
when a
leopard should
change
its spots.

You have
to put the
horse in
the harness
before it can
pull a plow.

Our greatest
possession
is today and
our greatest
heritage is
tomorrow.

You can't
have the
stew without
the oyster.

Very few things are right or wrong, they are usually just different.

Do not try to
distort my
dreams with what
you perceive to
be reality.

Greed is a narcotic
  of the spirit that
transcends logic,
  distorts perspective,
  and subverts
  loyalties.

Discipline the body
to purify the
spirit.

A reaction to
a problem is
rarely, if ever, the
solution.

Peace never destroyed
anything worth
preserving.

Happiness cannot
be given and
can be only
found within oneself.

The second law of
the jungle is survival
of those who
adapt best to
the changes
occurring around
them.

Philosophy is
the compass
of life.

The success of an
individual should
be measured by the
quality of character
and not by the amount
of material wealth
possessed.

Jealousy,
hate,
and anger
are the
enemies of
happiness.

To express my
dreams is
to release, in
part, the force
necessary to
bring them
to reality.

What
is real
to one
person
may not
be to
another.

The tree told me her
leaves were red and
gold; but when I
looked, they were
still green.

I must do the things
that make me,
me.

You are an integrity.
What someone
else is or is not can
neither detract
from you
or add to you.

The road to hell
and failure
is paved with
good intentions.

Wealth will not
bring happiness;
however, happiness
will let you
enjoy life regardless
of the amount
of wealth you have.

The escape route
from poverty
goes directly
through education.

One of the saddest
things in my life is
to want everyone to
be as happy as I am,
only to realize that
happiness
cannot be
given.

Pessimism is
a philosophical
disease.

I always
thought N
should come
before M
in the
alphabet.

A philosophy stated
and not practiced
is contemptible.

When we attempt to
solve a problem,
we must ensure the
solution does not
contain the seeds
of another
problem.

Some things we
learn should
be discarded
immediately
upon discovering
their true
nature.

What I do and
what I say is a
commentary
about me and
not about you.

Let the flower
warm you,
not the anger.

Talent does
what it can
and genius
does what it
has to.

Do not react
to the
absence
of
communication.

Preparation is
where the contest
is won or lost; the
outcome of the
engagement is
a mere formality.

The only thing
we must give up,
along with
our youth, is
our inexperience.

Since I continually
feel very good for
no specific reason,
this must be
a natural state...
and when I feel
bad, it is the
proximate result
of something I
did.

I once let someone
try to confine
me to a box built of
their expectations
of me and it literally
almost killed me.
I had to leave.

We must be careful,
when conforming
to the structures of
society, not to
lose our
own identity.

Happiness is like
knowledge, a
treasure that
cannot be
stolen.

The first step to
self-improvement
is being open
enough to
recognize that
you need it.

An inventor is an inventor because he thinks and does things differently.

One of the secrets of
running up a hill
is understanding that
you must plan to
run down the
other side in good
form.

If you only do the easy things, you will never experience the thrill of achievement.

Fulfillment of
life can only be
achieved by emptying
yourself for
others after
filling yourself
for you.

Do not criticize
yourself; others
will gladly do it
for you.
Your job
is to improve
yourself,
as you perceive
it to be

necessary.

If your conduct is
such that you
look, think,
and act like a
champion, you
are well on
the way to being one.

The first conquest
anyone should
make is
of oneself.

If someone asks for
help it may be
okay to refuse, but
for God's sake
do not throw them
a rock instead
of a lifesaver.

Relationships can
change and
need not end.

Within prudent
limits, accept
life's experiences at
face value.

The opposite side of
neglect is the
freedom to develop
as one chooses.

You cannot adjust
or adapt to a
situation by ignoring it,
but only by facing
it squarely
and rationally.

If we want to be
something we
are not, we must
first be willing
to give up
what we are.

The world always
looks better
over a bowl of
spaghetti.

Jails are a
testimony to
our failure
as parents,
citizens, and
society.

An inability is
not a weakness
until you fail to
compensate
for it.

Mental cruelty is the
equivalent of
physical cruelty,
except that one
damages the mind
and the other
damages the
body.

The truly powerful are
those who serve
their fellow
men; they are givers,
not takers.

Achievement is
realized through
challenge,
commitment,
control, effort,
pain, and sacrifice.

Love has many
forms of
expression.

We each have our
own paths to
walk; in as much
as we can, let us
walk them
together.

It is wonderful to
know where all of
the buttons are that
make your life
work; however,
it is something
else to have the
will to push
them at the proper
time.

Michaelangelo never
carved David
with one swing
of the hammer.

The difference between
a live and a dead
language is
that the live
language is
sensitive and
responsive to the
changes taking
place about it;
so should we
be.

Everyone is entitled
to their own
interpretation
of events.

Regardless of how
strong we are,
we all have a
breaking point,
and what carries us
beyond it is
faith and time.

In the
administration
of the law,
too many people
put their
personal
interests above
ensuring that
justice is
served.

You are going to
hurt during
a love affair, as
well as a marathon;
yet we enter
both willingly.

Greed was the first
sin and is the
source of all others,
and until you
overcome greed,
you will never have
peace in
your life.

Happiness can be
an elective state of
mind. Therefore,
why would anyone
choose to be
unhappy.

Trouble and misery
are only
perceptions. Therefore,
you only have them
if you perceive to
have them.

Expediency is the
precursor of
disaster.

If you truly love
someone, you
will not make your
love a burden
for that person.

Life is a series of
hurdles and it is
important to keep
in mind that
you can only jump
one at a time.

You do not mellow
with age; you
gain perspective.

Take pleasure
when you can,
since drudgery tends
to impose itself,
and pleasure
does not.

Do not ask someone
to be something
they are not.

One of the greatest
tragedies in life is
when a person
sacrifices health to
gain wealth, and
then attempts
to buy back the
health with
the wealth they
have gained.

People will only
change and improve
at their own
choosing.

You are alive as long
as you have a dream;
without a dream you
merely exist, as a
stone exists, and as
long as your
dream lives, you live.

Logic is not sacred,
   but you should not
deny its existence
   or be angry
with anyone who
   asks you
to face it.

A love affair can
continue without sex;
otherwise, there
was never
any love.

We will neither be
enhanced nor
diminished by comparing
ourselves to others.

Risk for its
own sake
is stupidity,
not courage.

One of the
best things
about being
over 50 is
that you have
many more
things to
celebrate than
you did
at 21.

Love's only
dictate
is to love.

Your mind, as
well as your
body, does what
you train it
to do.

I love you
but I cannot
imprison
myself in
that love.

Society is all
too accepting of
correcting problems
for which
they were
all too indifferent
about
preventing.

Anger and
greed are
the
archenemies
of logic
and
justice.

A person who
looks for
someone else
to give them
happiness
will only
find
disappointment.

When your feet
leave the ground
you lose control
of your body;
when you jump
to a
conclusion,
you lose
control of
your logic.

The spirit of
the universe
is immortal;
if we
can join that
spirit, we
will be
immortal.

There are those
among us
who, in order
to compensate
for their
insecurity,
go about
denigrating
others, hoping
to improve
their own
stature.

What you and
I are to
others has
nothing to do
with what
we are
to each other.

Set your goals
    high enough so
that there is a
    risk of
failure; otherwise,
you will never
    reach
    your full
potential.

It is very sad
to see
people who
seek
their identity
through
material possessions.

I would much
rather damage
myself with the
truth than
help
myself with
a lie.

It is more important
to concentrate on
what we are
than on what
we are not.

It is
I
who must
catch another
and not the
other who
must
wait for
me.

Everyone has
the right
to
self-determination
without
interference or
unwanted
and undue
criticism.

If you want
to wear
the mantle
of leadership,
you must
first
develop the
substance
of it.

Almost
everything can
be our ally
if we
permit it
to be.

Understanding of
other people starts
when you interpret the
relationship, on a
face-value basis,
in terms of
the other person's
situation and
not your own.

Incorrigibility
is a human
tendency.

Your strength,
as well as your
weakness, can
lead to your undoing.

Laws are
usually the
post-mortems
of tragedies.

The greatest power
on earth can never be
destructive ~
it is love.

Do not create something that is not there, and do not ignore something that is.

Somewhere today, there is an eagle soaring and a butterfly flying free rather than being stuffed and mounted or being pinned to a collector's board.

It is more
important to prevent
a mistake than to
criticize the
person who
made it.

Never ever,
ever,
ever be
self-demeaning.

If someone loves
you, do not
use that love to
make demands
of them.

The best gift you
can give a
child
is a
disciplined generosity.

Inner peace is
to be attained by
fulfilling
commitments to
oneself as well
as others.

There never was
and there never
will be any glory in
war or destruction.

Do not wear
life like
a
hairshirt.

Love is something
to be given
freely
and not bartered
for.

Dishonest people
perpetrate their greatest
fraud against
themselves.

The most important
things in life
are ethereal.
Therefore, life
is ethereal.

The province of
youth is to learn,
and not criticize.

Involve yourself
only with
positive thoughts,
endeavors, and
people.

Taste the infinite
sweetness of the present,
for it will never
come again.

It is not a secret
if two people
know it.

There is an empty space
in my life that is
not loneliness, but
a space that gives
me freedom to
move about to do
things and associate
with those that
I choose.

As long as
there is life,
there can be will.
If there is will,
there are
few limits.

There are
no one-way
streets in life.

To deny
something that
has existed
is to
deny part
of your own
existence.

I should have
ridden the
merry-go-round
and I should
have taken the
canoe ride.

It is very important
to remember who
washed whose feet
at the
last supper.

It is
only
important
that I
perceive
myself
as a
success.

The morals
of our society are
a reflection of
the ethics of
parents,
leaders, and
business people.

The door
of love only
opens from
the
inside.

Respect
territorial
imperatives.

It is not so important
if you lie to me or
if I lie to you,
but what is
important
is that you never
lie to you
and I
never lie to me.

To love is
not
to dominate.

Yesterday is
gone and
I do not live
there
anymore.

Looking at only the
negative aspects of
any situation is
equivalent to only
eating the bad spot
in an apple.

Glory is like frost
upon the glass,
in that as the sun
rises to expose
its existence, by the
very act, melts
it away.

We only
belong to
ourselves.

Each of us is the
steward of our
own talents and
bears the
responsibility for
their developement
and use.

A first impression
must be validated
with a test for
substance.

The power of
one can be more
easily understood
when you think
of Christ.

If Michaelangelo
would have
been married,
the world would
have been denied
some of its
beauty.

Coffee has been
my only life
long love affair.

Once you have
done all you can
reasonably do
about a situation,
there is no
longer any
reason
to
worry about
the outcome.

You can't force
the flower
to bloom, you can
only provide the
environment.

Materialists
live in the
past.

In thought, there
is no final
conclusion.